HackneyandJones.com

Writers and Publishers

HACKNEY & JONES

Grab your freebies at

HackneyandJones.com

SCAN ME

THE COMPLETE ONLINE COURSE DESIGN WORKBOOK

CREATE ONLINE COURSES FROM SCRATCH

Hackney and Jones

INTRODUCTION

We are Claire Hackney and Vicky Jones, and together we have created Hackney and Jones Publishing. Over the last five years we have created, written and published over 1400 books (fiction non-fiction) including notebooks, planners, journals and kid's activity books through platforms such as Amazon and Ingram Spark. Everything we have learned from our exciting journey through self-publishing has equipped us with the knowledge and understanding of what makes a great product.

This is why we have put together this workbook - to provide you with the information needed to create the perfect online course, not just to help you make money, but to ensure the content you are creating for your customers hits the mark and gets them to their goal in the best, most efficient and informative way possible.

Within the pages of this workbook you will find advice taken from our experience, and valuable content you can learn from to adopt in your own processes. There are also templates for you to use when you are at the stage of putting together your own course programme.

So, let's make a start with the first chapter.

We wish you all the best

WHY YOU ARE HERE

We hear you. You want to know what to create a course about, but are unsure of how to get started on your chosen topic.

You also want to earn some serious cash and need to know which topic would be best, and then you need help with how to research and put it all together.

The WHOLE of your success comes down to:

Does your course solve a problem?

Yes, it really is THAT simple.

How do we know what the problems are?

We research.

By giving your audience EXACTLY what they want (which we will find out via the research methods in this workbook, your course will succeed).

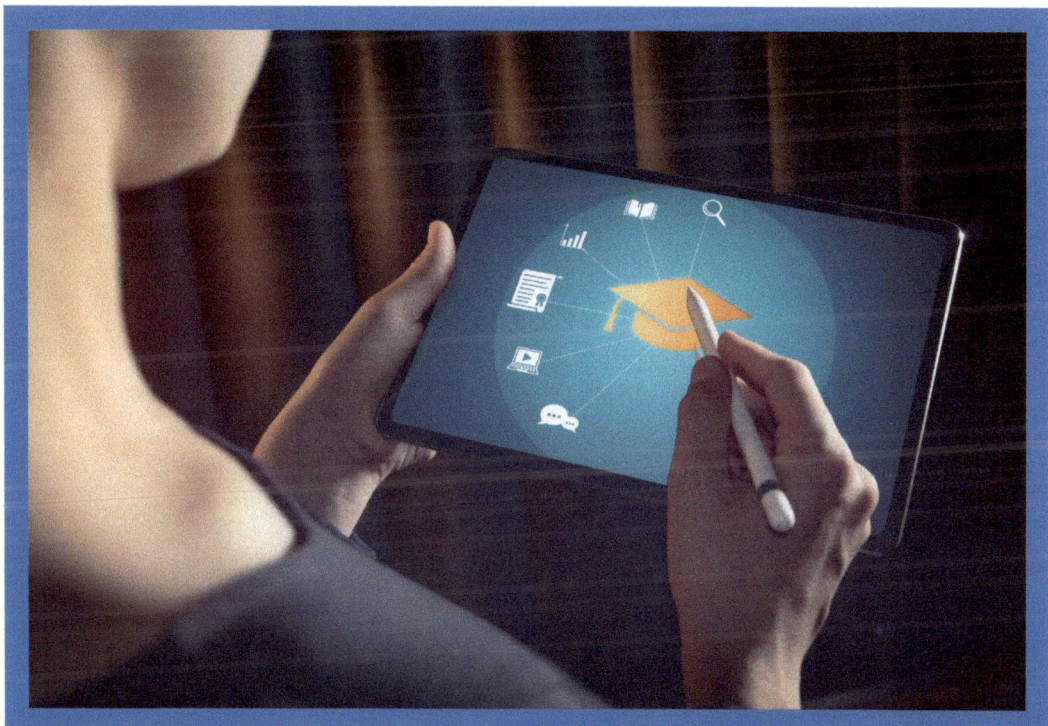

WHAT TO EXPECT

This book has been specifically designed to remove all of the fluff that other workbooks tend to include before they get to the useful stuff. We understand your time is valuable and aim to cut straight to the content that is going to help you succeed in your online course design project. No fluff, no fillers and certainly no fuss.

So, as promised, let's skip to the good bit...

What we will cover in this workbook:

- **What to expect** - Why you are here and why you need to plan your course this way.

- **Let's create!** - How to come up with the content for your course.

- **Your lesson plans** - How to ensure you only include what is essential.

- **What do I do now?** - How to organise your content into a logical order and ensure your student achieves their goal.

- **Copywriting** - The secrets to selling your course!

- **Resources** - Have everything you need to succeed!

BRAINSTORM TIME

Brainstorm ALL the possible ideas you have for an online course.

Don't think about it, don't edit, just write!

YOUR EMAIL LIST

Send an email to your email list and ask them what their **MAIN** problems/pain points are and what they would **LOVE** as a solution.

Tick the box once you have done this

TOP 5 ANSWERS

1.

2.

3.

4.

5.

YOUR TWITTER/INSTAGRAM/FACEBOOK AUDIENCE

Send an email to your email list and ask them what their MAIN problems/pain points are and what they would LOVE as a solution.

Tick the box once you have done this

TOP 5 ANSWERS

1.

2.

3.

4.

5.

YOUR VIEWS

What are you passionate about and what do people regularly ask you for advice about? Use this information to decide your top 3 ideas for what your online course could be about.

PEOPLE ASK ME ABOUT........

BECAUSE.......

PEOPLE ASSOCIATE ME WITH BEING THE PERSON WHO.....

BECAUSE.......

MY PASSIONS IN LIFE ARE......

WHAT I KNOW A LOT ABOUT.....

LESSONS I HAVE LEARNED IN MY LIFE...

MY TOP 3 ONLINE COURSE IDEAS:

1.

2.

3.

IS YOUR COURSE IDEA ANY GOOD?

It's time to do some research into whether your idea is popular with the rest of the world. This is incredibly important to do as you do not want to be wasting your time creating an awesome online course if no one on the planet is asking for it.

Rule one of making money is to "find a need and fill it, find a problem and solve it."

Firstly, type 'Google Trends' into Google search engine.

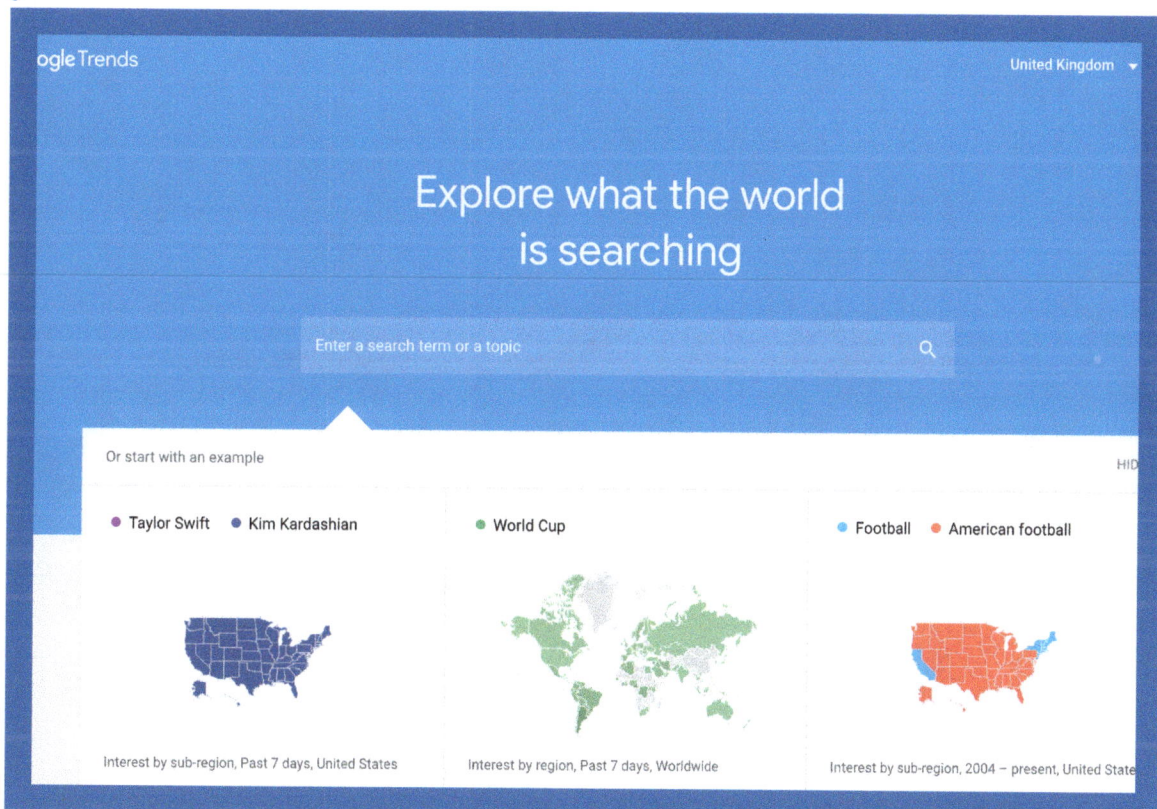

Google Trends will tell you how popular your idea is depending on your country. You will be able to tell if it's a niche worth going after. If it has a continual downward 'trend' maybe you should look at something else.

An upward or constant trend is what you are looking for.

HOW POPULAR IS YOUR ONLINE COURSE IDEA WITH THE REST OF THE WORLD?

An example: 'HOW TO BAKE A CAKE'

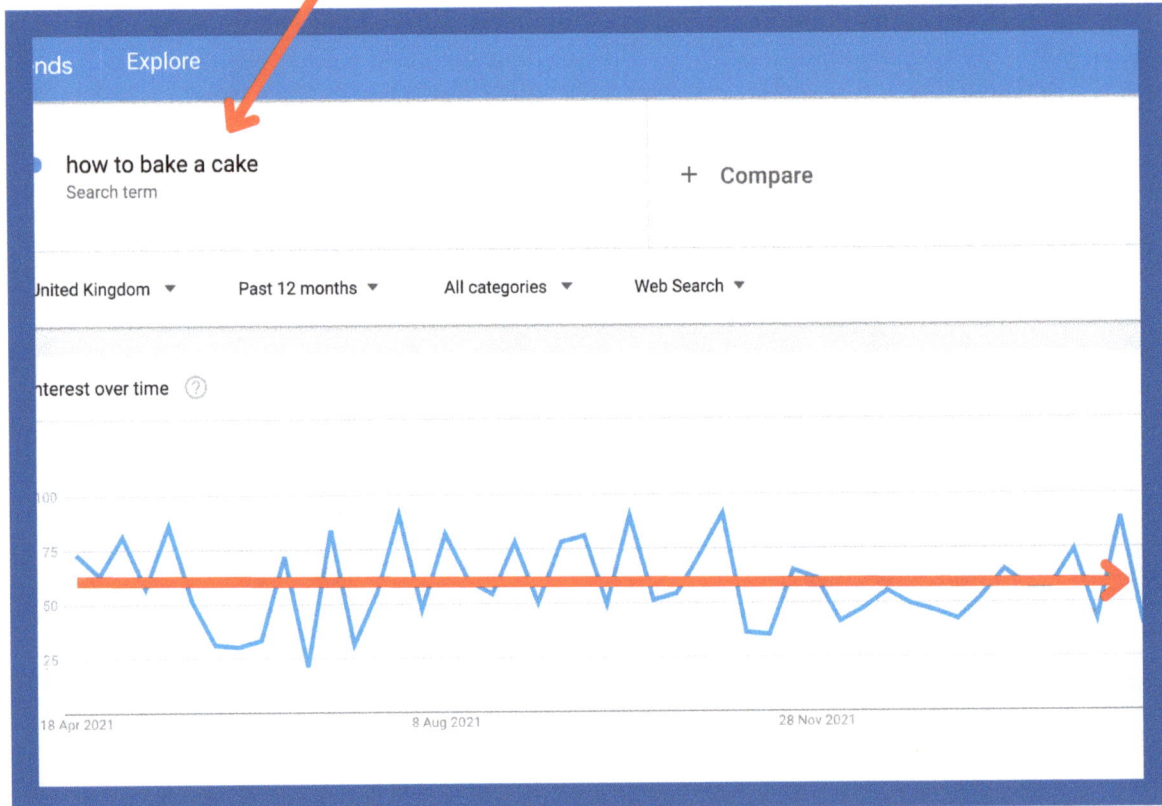

This is a pretty 'evergreen' niche ie. it's popular throughout the year. This would be worth exploring further - or niching down further as it is quite broad.

HOW POPULAR IS YOUR ONLINE COURSE IDEA WITH THE REST OF THE WORLD?

Type in each of your Top 3 Online Course ideas to Google Trends to see how popular each one is and which months it is MOST popular.

The best course to start with is for it to be 'evergreen' ie. popular throughout the year.

MY TOP 3 ONLINE COURSE IDEAS:

IDEA 1.

MONTHS THIS IDEA IS THE MOST POPULAR:

IDEA 2.

MONTHS THIS IDEA IS THE MOST POPULAR:

IDEA 3.

MONTHS THIS IDEA IS THE MOST POPULAR:

BUT WHICH ONLINE COURSE IS THE BEST CHOICE?

Use the 'compare' feature on Google Trends and add each idea and see how they compare against each other.

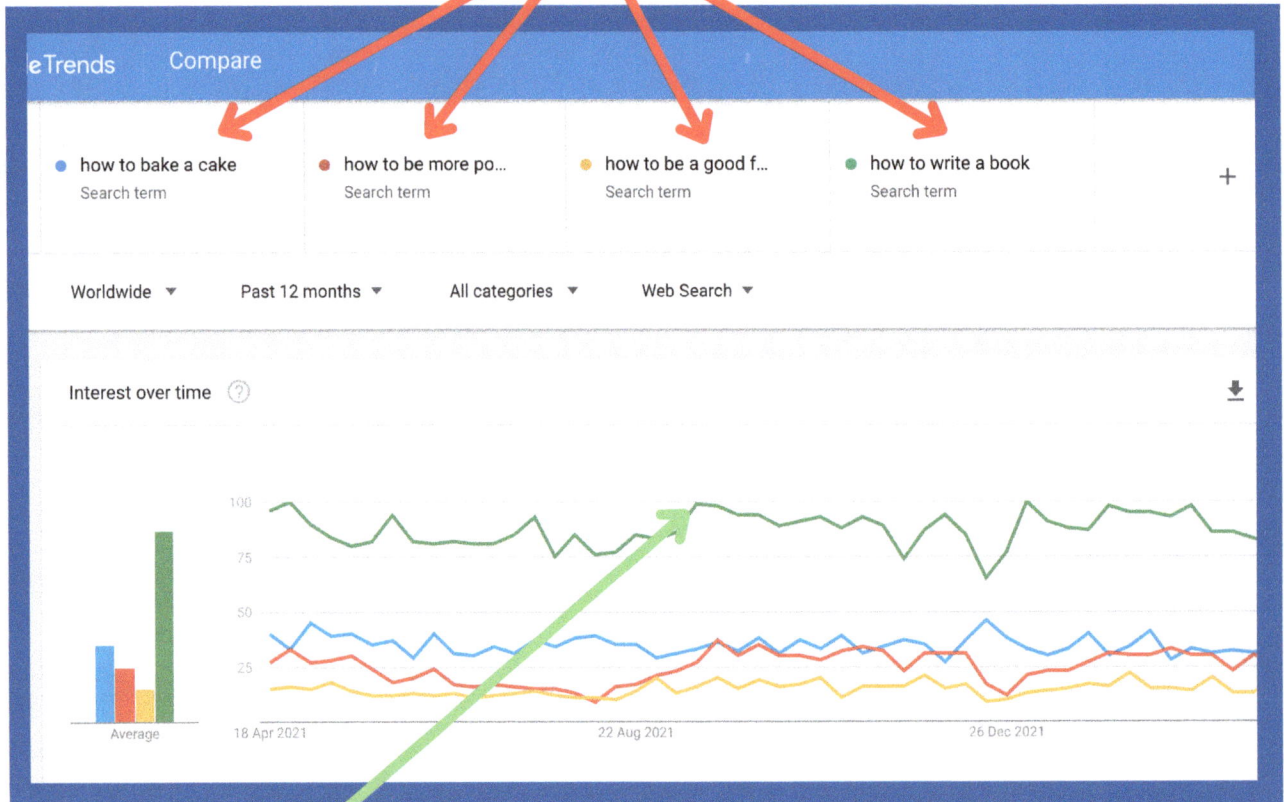

The GREEN line is my idea for 'How To Write A Book.'

It looks pretty good, doesn't it?

Out of all of my 'ideas', it has the MOST search volume and is evergreen which means it is getting searched for all year round.

YOUR TURN

Enter your BEST ideas into Google Trends 'Compare.'

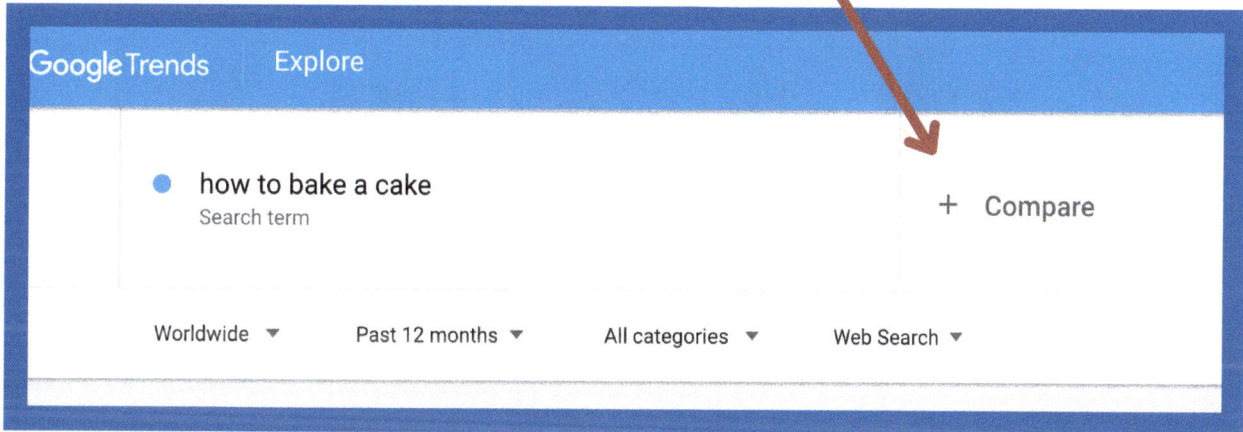

Which online course idea overall is BEST? Write it below:

MY OVERALL BEST CHOICE OF COURSE IS:

YOUR ONLINE COURSE IDEA

MY COURSE IS ALL ABOUT:

I FEEL I CAN CREATE A COURSE ABOUT THIS BECAUSE:

BRAIN DUMP

WRITE DOWN ALL OF THE THINGS YOU THINK YOU NEED TO COVER IN THIS COURSE - DON'T EDIT, JUST WRITE!

1.

2.

3.

4.

5.

6.

7.

8.

9.

10.

GOOGLE SEARCH FOR IDEAS

Let's pretend my niche is 'How to bake a cake.'

PRESS THE SPACE BAR but DON'T PRESS RETURN JUST YET.

Type into Google - 'Ways to....' (and add your niche).

G   ways to bake a cake

🔍   ways to bake a cake - Google Search

🔍   ways to bake a cake **without an oven**

🔍   **4** ways to bake a cake

🔍   **different** ways to bake a cake

🔍   **easy** ways to bake a cake

🔍   **other** ways to bake a cake

🔍   **alternative** ways to bake a cake

🔍   ways to bake a **chocolate** cake

🔍   ways to **make** a **box** cake

🔍   ways to bake cake **mix**

I may not have even thought about this as an idea. But it is one of the most searched for queries in my niche.

GOOGLE SEARCH FOR IDEAS

Let's pretend my niche is '**How to bake a cake.**'

PRESS THE SPACE BAR but **DON'T PRESS RETURN JUST YET.**

Type into Google - 'How to....' (and add your niche).

G   how to bake a cake |

🔍   how to bake a cake - Google Search

🔍   how to bake a cake **step by step**

🔍   how to bake a cake **in an air fryer**

🔍   how to bake a cake **without eggs**

🔍   how to bake a cake **in minecraft**

This will be one of the most searched for queries on Google that is related to my niche.

ALPHABET SOUP

We want to niche down a bit so that our course isn't too broad as we will be swamped with the competition.

Type into Google - 'Ways to....' (and add your niche) and add the letter 'A'
PRESS SPACE BAR (NOT RETURN)

G   ways to bake a cake a

Q   ways to bake a cake a - Google Search

Q   **how** to bake a cake a**t home**

MOST POPULAR

Q   **how** to bake a cake a**nd ingredients**

Q   **how** to bake a cake **using** a **jiko**

Q   **how long** to bake a cake a**t 180**

G   ways to bake a cake b|

NOW USE THE LETTER 'B'

Q   ways to bake a cake b - Google Search

Q   **how** to bake a cake b**y scratch**

MOST POPULAR

Q   **how** to bake a cake b**irthday**

Q   **how** to bake a cake b**lack forest**

Q   **how** to bake a b**anana** cake

Q   **how** to bake a b**utter** cake

ALPHABET SOUP

Do the 'Alphabet' soup for every letter of the alphabet for:

Ways to... (your niche)

AND

How to...(your niche)

Write down ALL of the TOP queries for each one on the next page.

ALPHABET SOUP

Write down the MOST popular Google search terms in your niche from doing the alphabet soup (that you are interested in).

MOST POPULAR GOOGLE SEARCH TERMS FROM ALPHABET SOUP RESEARCH

1.

2.

3.

4.

5.

6.

7.

8.

9.

10.

11.

12.

ALPHABET SOUP

Pick the **TOP 10** you would be interested in creating a course about.

Write the **'Google search volume'** in the box next to it.

To get the Google search volume, you can use websites such as **'Uber suggest'** or my personal favourite, **google keyword planner** below (this is FREE).

ALPHABET SOUP

'How to bake a cake' is getting searched for around 60,500 times a month!

Keyword (by relevance)	Vol	CPC	Comp	Trend	Avg. monthly searches
Keywords you provided					
how to bake a cake ★	60,500	$0.55	0.09		1K – 10K
Keyword ideas					
how to make banana cake ★	14,800	$0.32	0.09		1K – 10K
how to make cake at home ★	14,800	$0.39	0.09		100 – 1K
how to make sponge cake ★	12,100	$0.31	0.06		1K – 10K
how to make a cake from scratch ★	8,100	$1.30	0.05		100 – 1K
how to bake a simple cake for beginners ★	5,400	$0.33	0.07		100 – 1K
how to make vanilla cake ★	9,900	$1.23	0.04		1K – 10K
how to make cheese cake ★	2,200	$0.69	0.1		10K – 100K
how to make a simple cake ★	4,400	$0.68	0.08		100 – 1K

We may even like some of these other ideas that Google has given us. Write down their search volume too.

A search term of 60,500 a month will be swamped with competition, so our course may not even get seen :(

ALPHABET SOUP

Write down the MOST popular Google search terms in your niche from doing the alphabet soup (that you are interested in).

SEARCH VOLUME FROM ALPHABET SOUP RESEARCH

1.   SEARCH VOLUME:

2.   SEARCH VOLUME:

3.   SEARCH VOLUME:

4.   SEARCH VOLUME:

5.   SEARCH VOLUME:

6.   SEARCH VOLUME:

7.   SEARCH VOLUME:

8.   SEARCH VOLUME:

9.   SEARCH VOLUME:

10.   SEARCH VOLUME:

PICK THE ONE BEST FOR YOU

You want to make money, right?

But you also want to create a course that you have an interest about too.

So, out of the 10 ideas you have written down, take into consideration their search volume (the higher the better) and your interest in them, and write down the course you want to create below. Be mindful that the higher the search volume, the more competition you will up against. But we are going to create an amazing course, right?

....

Don't forget, if you have discovered more ideas for courses, you can come back and do the same process for those!

The more courses, the better = more money for you!

CAN WE NICHE DOWN EVEN MORE?

'But I want to appeal to EVERYBODY'

The reason why niching down is better for you (especially at the start of your journey) is so you have a better chance of appearing first, whether it be Google, Pinterest etc. because there is less competition. Eg. your phrase may only get 500 searches per month, but you have a higher chance of appearing near the top for that than trying to compete for 'How to Bake a Cake' that may have 60,000 searches a month. where it will be swamped with the competition.

How do I niche down further?

Put the symbol _ before you type your course name into 'Google'. Then do the 'alphabet soup' if you like to get more ideas.

This will then ensure that longer keywords will show up.

Example:

G   _ how to make a cake at home without an oven

Q   _ how to make a cake at home without an oven - Google Search

Q   how to make a cake at home without an oven

Q   how to make a **simple** cake at home without an oven

Q   how to make a cake without using an oven

Q   how to make **small** cake at home without oven

Q   **can i** make a cake without an oven

We know this is getting searched for, it's telling us what the customer wants 'simple, no bake, and be able to make at home'.

CAN WE NICHE DOWN EVEN MORE?

'Write down your Top 3 niched down titles here:
(Our example would be 'How to make a simple cake at home without an oven'.

Look up their search volume on Google (where we looked before).

1 .... Search volume ....

2 .... Search volume ....

3 .... Search volume ....

Now go onto 'Google Trends' like we did before to see which options out of the 3 above is the best idea to go with:

Write it down here:

....

CAN WE NICHE DOWN EVEN MORE?

I would pick the 'blue' one as it's the MOST popular and seems to be evergreen.

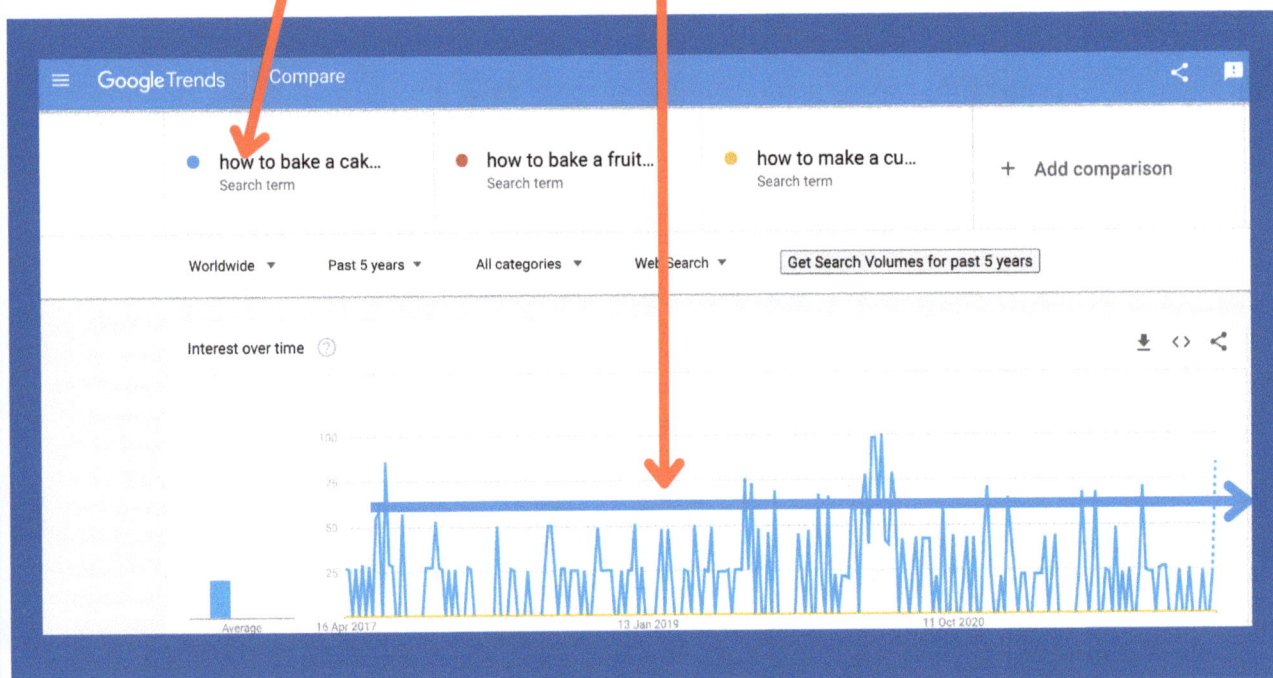

Our Winner is:

How to Bake a Cake Without an Oven

WHAT WILL BE THE TITLE OF YOUR ONLINE COURSE?

Your research is complete, so now you should know the best, most marketable title for your online course - it is the answer to the question most people are asking online; the need that needs to be met, the solution to a popular problem.

Write down the idea that has come out on top after all of your research.

THE SUBJECT/TITLE OF MY BRILLIANT ONLINE COURSE IS:

....

YOUR COURSE CONTENT

'Now we need to make sure our course contains what our audience wants.

How do we find this out?

Easy.

Head over to Quora.com (which is a question and answer website). In the questions section, type in your course idea like I did below:

Click on 'Questions' and you will only get what you need.

Type in question here.

Use the questions as a possible idea for sub-headings/lessons.
Use the answers as inspiration (DO NOT COPY).

YOUR COURSE CONTENT

Use websites such as 'Answer the Public' to find out what else people are searching for.

By including the answers to these queries/questions in YOUR course, you will be giving incredible value!

Can you see how many questions people ask about YOUR course?

Obviously, not all will be relevant, but use your 'Post-It's for all the ideas you think would be a good lesson/video.

YOUR COURSE CONTENT

Modifier	Suggestion
are	how to bake a cake without an oven
are	how to bake a cake without an oven in uganda
are	how to make a cake without an oven
are	how to cook a cake without an oven
are	how to bake a chocolate cake without an oven
are	how to bake a sponge cake without an oven
are	how to bake a banana cake without an oven
are	how to bake a cake without oven and pressure cooker
can	how to bake a cake without an oven
can	how to bake a cake without an oven in uganda
can	how to make a cake without an oven
can	how to cook a cake without an oven
can	how to bake a chocolate cake without an oven
can	how to bake a sponge cake without an oven
can	how to bake a banana cake without an oven
can	how to bake a cake without oven and pressure cooker
how	how to bake a cake without an oven
how	how to bake a cake without an oven in uganda
how	how to make a cake without an oven
how	how to cook a cake without an oven
how	how to bake a chocolate cake without an oven
how	how to bake a sponge cake without an oven
how	how to bake a banana cake without an oven

These can be individual lessons.

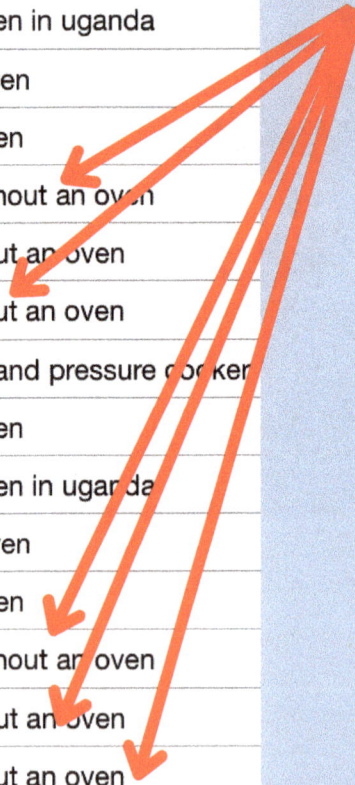

LET'S CREATE!

Type the name of your course into Google and press RETURN.

Scroll down to where it says 'People also ask' and on your Post-it notes, write down the questions you find.

My example for 'Ways to make a no bake cake'

People also ask ⋮

How can we make cake at home without oven?

How do you make a no bake candy cake?

How do you bake a cake in the freezer?

These 'could' be your subheadings/lessons if they are relevant.

LET'S CREATE!

Scroll to the VERY BOTTOM of the same Google page.

You will see some more things people are asking Google, which means we want these in our course (if relevant).

Write down these ideas.

They could be separate lessons...? Eg. a section on '5-minute cakes', or '3 ingredient cakes' etc.

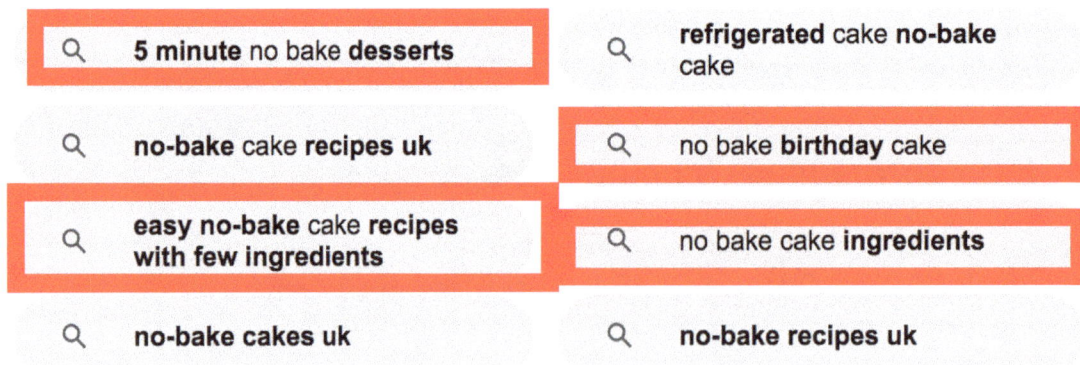

🔍 **5 minute** no bake **desserts**	🔍 **refrigerated** cake **no-bake** cake
🔍 **no-bake** cake recipes uk	🔍 no bake **birthday** cake
🔍 **easy no-bake** cake **recipes with few ingredients**	🔍 no bake cake **ingredients**
🔍 **no-bake cakes** uk	🔍 **no-bake recipes** uk

Goooooooooogle ›

1 2 3 4 5 6 7 8 9 10   Next

LET'S CREATE!

Type your course name into **Google** and press return.

Make a note of anything that catches your eye on the first 1-2 pages from your search.

These articles/blogs etc. are popular because people are wanting the information contained in them.

DO NOT COPY exact titles.

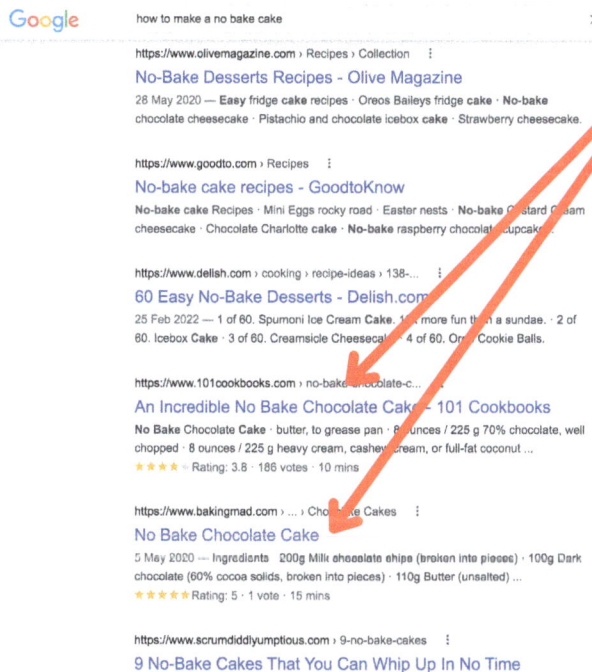

I definitely need to include a chocolate cake in my course as it has appeared twice in the titles of the first page.

On separate 'Post-It' notes, start making a note of the keywords/adverbs etc. that will be vital for our copy later on.

It will give us a more punchy heading.

Such as: 'Easy', 'incredible', 'whip-up' etc.

LET'S CREATE!

Head over to Pinterest.

Go to the search bar and type out your niche/course idea and at first, **DON'T PRESS RETURN** and see what appears.

Write down **EVERYTHING** that you feel would be relevant for **YOUR** course. Here, it seems like people would want to know the step-by-step approach to baking, so I would write down 'step by step' as we can also use that for our sales copy later.

how to bake a cake without an oven

- Q how to bake cake without oven
- Q how to bake cake without an oven
- Q how to bake cake step by step without oven
- Q how to bake cake without oven video
- Q how to bake chocolate cake without oven
- Q how to bake eggless cake without oven

YOUR COURSE CONTENT

Head over to Amazon.

Type the name of your course in the search bar.

I had to be inventive and change some of my keywords.

| Books ▼ | how to bake a cake without an oven |

I learned that I would get more relevant books if I typed in 'No bake cakes'.

YOUR COURSE CONTENT

I looked at the titles/subtitles of **'No Bake cakes'**.

Look up the top 5-10 bestselling books in your niche.

RESULTS

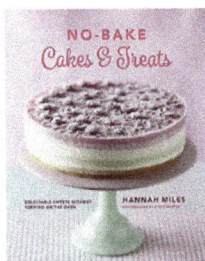

No-Bake! Cakes & Treats Cookbook: Delectable Sweets Without Turning on the Oven
by Hannah Miles | 30 Apr 2016
★★★☆☆ ⌄ 21
Hardcover
£8¹⁹ £9.99
50% off gift wrap service: code GIFTWRAP50
Get it **Tomorrow, Apr 17**
FREE Delivery on your first order shipped by Amazon
Only 5 left in stock (more on the way).
More buying choices
£2.35 (27 used & new offers)

Best Seller

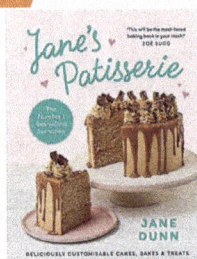

Sponsored ⓘ
Jane's Patisserie: Deliciously customisable cakes, bakes and treats. THE NO.1 SUNDAY TIMES BESTSELLER
by Jane Dunn | 5 Aug 2021
★★★★★ ⌄ 6,717
Hardcover
£10⁰⁰ £20.00
50% off gift wrap service: code GIFTWRAP50
✓prime Get it **Tomorrow, Apr 17**
FREE Delivery by Amazon

Sponsored ⓘ
My Kitchen Table: 100 Cakes and Bakes (My Kitchen, 10)
by Mary Berry | 6 Jan 2011
★★★★½ ⌄ 5,482
Paperback
£7.68

YOUR COURSE CONTENT

Write down any ideas that you think would be beneficial to your online course on your 'Post-Its'.

Copy and paste ALL 5-10 bestselling titles and descriptions in 'Word'.

Type into Google 'Word Frequency Counter'

I personally use Helium 10 Frankenstein which is AMAZING for this.

Your goal is to find which words are included the MOST in the bestselling titles and descriptions.

Let me show you...

Get Helium 10 here (with a discount)

SCAN ME

YOUR COURSE CONTENT

31	recipes
19	cheesecake
18	cookbook
13	cakes
13	sweet
12	no
9	oven
9	book
9	cheesecakes
9	cake
9	making
9	have
8	dessert
8	can
8	will
7	time
7	no-bake
7	bake
6	treats
6	chocolate
5	ingredients
5	fridge
5	desserts
5	simple
5	make
5	pies
4	baking
4	party
	require

So you can see which words feature the MOST in our bestselling 'no bake' books.

Use a 'Post-It' note and write down the top content ideas such as:

- **Cheesecake**
- **Sweet**
- **Chocolate**
- **Treats**
- **Pies** etc.

Then, make a note of all of the 'copywriting' words (the words that will help 'sell' your course).

For our example, I would write:

- **recipes**
- **simple**
- **party etc.**

I know my audience wants simple recipes for treats and parties.

Get Helium 10 here (with a discount)

[QR code: SCAN ME]

YOUR COURSE CONTENT

Pick 5- 10 of the bestsellers on Amazon that are in your niche.

Click on each one and now look at the REVIEWS:

⭐⭐⭐⭐⭐ **Dessert lovers and no-bake lovers rejoice - this cookbook is for YOU!**
Reviewed in the United States on 26 July 2016
<u>Verified Purchase</u>

I am absolutely in love with this cookbook!! Living in Phoenix, AZ where summer temperatures can reach 115° F. the less I turn the oven on, the better. Julianne's cookbook has a variety of recipes that will appeal to everyone. Whether you're a chocolate, lemon, mint or fruit lover there are recipes for you plus so much more. Each recipe has a gorgeous photo to go along with it making it even more difficult to decide which to make first.
I made the Hot Mess Nutella Snickers Cheesecake and it was phenomenal! My family loved the combination of the Oreo crust, Nutella filling, salted caramel, Snickers, peanut and whipped cream. It's definitely a dessert we won't soon forget!
Julianne's recipes are easy to follow, and I love that she's also included a tips and tool section. From the crust to the whipped cream to the garnish, she'll make sure that you're using and preparing the ingredients the right way to make your dessert perfect.
This is one cookbook I know that I'll be using over and over again. I've been excited to share it with others because I know they'll love it just as much as I do!

Things I should include in my content:

- **Variety of recipes.**
- **Chocolate, lemon, mint or fruit lover there are recipes for you.**
- **Each recipe has a gorgeous photo.**
- **Recipes are easy to follow.**
- **Included a tips and tool section.**

This is just 1 of MANY reviews! The data is pure gold!

YOUR COURSE CONTENT

The GOOD stuff!

Go through ALL of the 4-5 star reviews and write what was GOOD and make sure you include that here:

What I NEED to do/include in my course (from 4-5 star reviews).

....
....
....
....
....
....
....
....
....
....
....
....
....
....
....

YOUR COURSE CONTENT

The BAD stuff!

Go through ALL of the 1-3 star reviews and write what was BAD.

See my example:

★★☆☆☆ **Far too sweet, even for 'sweet treats' !!**
Reviewed in Germany on 11 August 2016
Verified Purchase

Unfortunately I am very disappointed with this book! I have read through it and find it very 'americanised'. I have not made anything but the recipes seem overly sweet.

The section on crispy treats consists of 'cakes' made with all kinds of breakfast cereal which are laden with sugar and additives, not in line with today's ideas of healthy eating.

I will be returning the book as it's not something I would ever use.

I would make sure that I included fewer sweet treats and also included some more savoury treats too.

YOUR COURSE CONTENT

The BAD stuff!

Go through ALL of the 1-3 star reviews and write what was BAD and make sure you include that here:

What I should AVOID in my course (from 1-3 star reviews)

....
....
....
....
....
....
....
....
....
....
....
....
....
....
....
....

YOUR COURSE CONTENT

By looking at the bestsellers in your niche, you will be seeing what works, and then do better.

The key is to give your customer exactly what they want...and more!

Get Helium 10 here (with a discount).

YOUR COURSE CONTENT

Pick your favourite 5-10 books again and click on the 'Look inside' button for each book and scroll to the contents page.

Look **inside** ↓

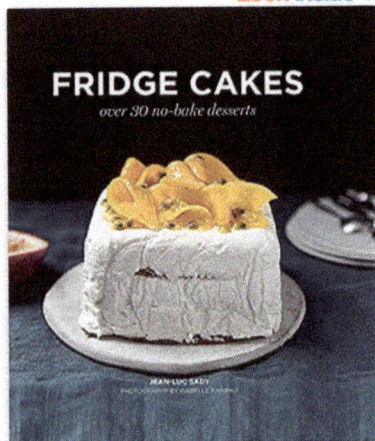

Fridge Cakes: Over 30 no-bake desserts

Hardcover – 6 April 2017

by Jean-Luc Sady (Author)

★★★★☆ ∨   19 ratings

See all formats and editions

Hardcover
£5.71

19 Used from £0.55
8 New from £2.91

CONTENTS

DO NOT COPY!

You are simply looking for inspiration as to what is popular/wanted from the bestselling books in your course niche. If you deliver this and more... and better, you are onto a WINNER!

YOUR COURSE CONTENT

Go on to Twitter 🐦

Go on to 'explore' with the hashtag symbol and type in your niche.

🐦

⌂ Home

\# Explore

🔔 ⑤ Notifications

✉ Messages

🔖 Bookmarks

▤ Lists

👤 **Profile**

⋯ More

Tweet

Knocked up very quickly my **no bake** strawberry cheese **cake**, once set its calling out from the fridge to be eaten

💬 3   ↺ 3   ♡ 13   ⬆

Lou Lou Girls @thelougirls · Apr 13
Triple Berry Poke **Cake** is a classic **cake** & fill with homemade berry sauce before topping with a tangy, delicious **no-bake** cheesecake! This **cake** is best made the day before, which makes it great to bring to all those summer potlucks! louougirls.com/2022/04/triple... #pokecake #desserts #yum

Homemade **no bake** choc **cake**. Mmm

Click on the 'top' tweet. That normally means it is the MOST popular. Look at what it is, what the comments are etc.

This can give you lots of ideas for your niche.

YOUR COURSE CONTENT

Go on to Twitter

Go on to 'explore' with the hashtag symbol and type in your niche.

What are some ideas that you have found on Twitter?:

....

....

....

....

....

....

....

....

....

....

Now, post on your Twitter the following:

'What are your biggest frustrations with..... (your niche)?'

Tick the box when you have done this ☐

YOUR COURSE CONTENT

Go on to Twitter

What are some of the frustrations that your audience had/have?

....

....

....

....

....

....

....

....

....

....

....

....

....

....

YOUR COURSE CONTENT

Go on to Facebook

Tick the box when you have done this ☐

Post in any groups that you are already a member of (sometimes you may need the permission of the admin, some you can post freely).

What are some of the frustrations that your audience had/have?

....

....

....

....

....

....

....

....

....

....

....

YOUR COURSE CONTENT

Go on to Facebook

Type your niche into the search bar under Groups and join as many as you can.

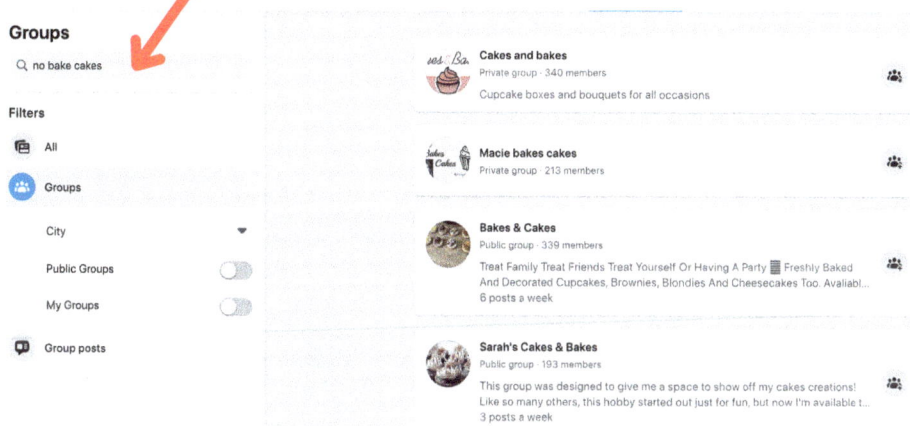

Once you have been accepted in the groups, start looking at common questions or 'pain points' that people have.

Your course needs to solve these pain points.

Post your 'What are your biggest frustrations with...?' (your niche) in your new groups and take a screenshot or write down all the answers and keep them safe. Even the wording will be excellent for your sales copy as you will be speaking the same language as your potential customers. Post 'what would be your IDEAL solution to...? (pain point in your niche).

YOUR COURSE CONTENT

Go on to Facebook

Common questions/answers to your questions from Facebook Groups that you need to include in your course:

....

....

....

....

....

....

....

....

....

....

....

....

....

....

YOUR COURSE CONTENT

Go on to YouTube

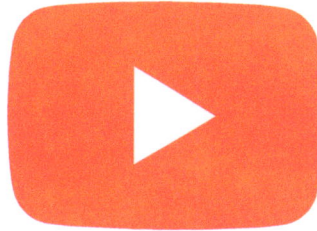

Type your niche into the search bar and do 'Alphabet soup' and see what comes up.

▶ YouTube GB

🔍 no bake cakes d

- 🔍 no bake **simple dessert**
- 🔍 no bake **dog treats**
- 🔍 no bake **dog treats recipe**
- 🔍 no bake cakes **and desserts**
- 🔍 **diy** cakes no bake

- 🏠 Home
- 🧭 Explore
- ⚡ Shorts
- ▣ Subscriptions

▶ YouTube GB

🔍 no bake cakes h

- 🏠 Home
- 🧭 Explore

- 🔍 no bake **hamster treats**
- 🔍 **how to make** no bake cakes

▶ YouTube GB

🔍 no bake cakes a

- 🏠 Home
- 🧭 Explore
- ⚡ Shorts

- 🔍 no bake cakes and **desserts**
- 🔍 no bake cakes and **slices**
- 🔍 no bake cakes and **pies**

Obviously, some of these may not be relevant, but COULD be ideas for other courses!

Write them down and put them to one side.

YOUR COURSE CONTENT

Go on to YouTube

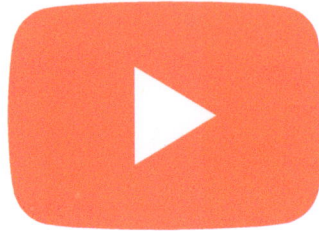

Type your niche into the search bar and do 'Alphabet soup' and see what comes up.

Ideas from YouTube:

....

....

....

....

....

....

....

....

....

....

....

....

....

YOUR COURSE CONTENT

Go on to YouTube

Type your niche into the search bar and then go onto 'filter'.

Look at the titles of the MOST VIEWED videos and write down their titles/content etc.

If these are popular, it's because there is DEMAND.

If your course includes these things, it will do awesome!

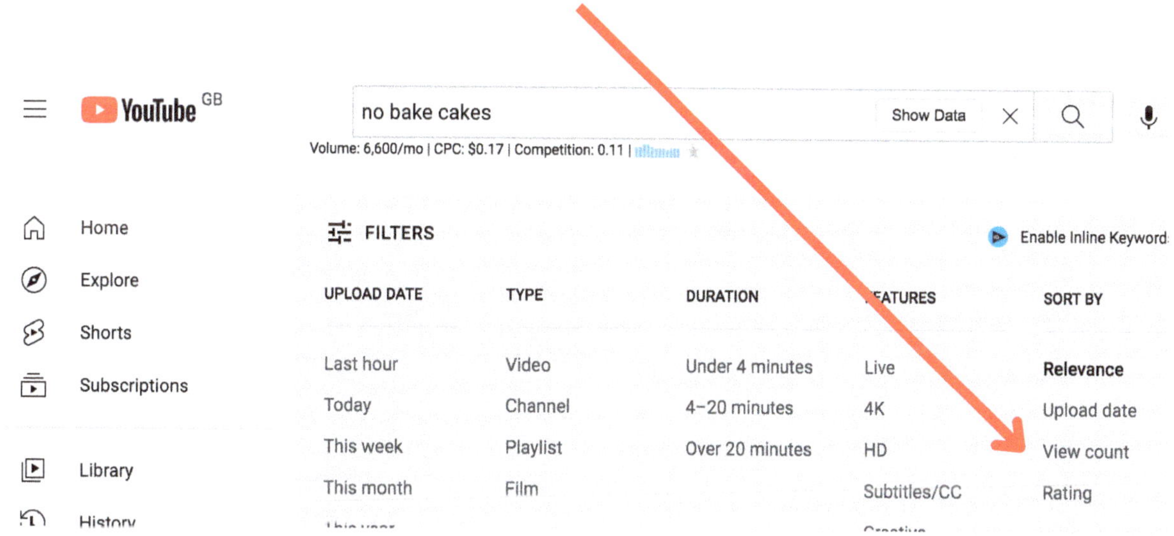

☰ ▶ YouTube GB	no bake cakes		Show Data ✕ 🔍 🎤	
	Volume: 6,600/mo	CPC: $0.17	Competition: 0.11				

🏠 Home	⚏ FILTERS			▶ Enable Inline Keyword
🧭 Explore				
🎵 Shorts	UPLOAD DATE	TYPE	DURATION	FEATURES	SORT BY
▣ Subscriptions	Last hour	Video	Under 4 minutes	Live	**Relevance**
	Today	Channel	4–20 minutes	4K	Upload date
▣ Library	This week	Playlist	Over 20 minutes	HD	View count
	This month	Film		Subtitles/CC	Rating
� History	This year			Creative	

YOUR COURSE CONTENT

Go on to YouTube

This was the number 1 viewed video in our niche. We NEED to include a Vanilla Sponge cake!

Easy Vanilla Sponge Cake Without Oven Recipe | How To Make Basic Sponge Cake | Plain Sponge Cake

This was the second most viewed. We NEED to include a simple chocolate cake in our course (that only has very few ingredients).

No Oven Chocolate Cake [Only 3 Ingredients]

YOUR COURSE CONTENT

Go on to YouTube

Write down the top 10-15 MOST viewed videos in your niche.

Make note of the title and anything else it includes that inspires you for YOUR course:

....

....

....

....

....

....

....

....

....

....

....

....

....

YOUR COURSE CONTENT

Go on to YouTube

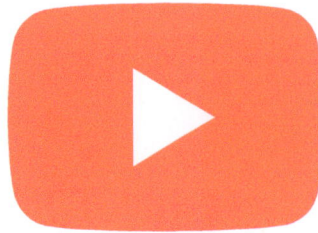

We are going to be looking at what our DIRECT COMPETITORS are doing with THEIR courses.

Go onto Udemy   ûdemy

Type in your niche:

ûdemy   Categories   🔍 no bake cakes

5,365 results for "no bake cakes"

Click on 5-10 of the bestselling and/or with the MOST reviews.

YOUR COURSE CONTENT

We are going to be looking at what our **DIRECT COMPETITORS** are doing with **THEIR** courses.

Go onto Udemy:

ûdemy

Type in your niche:

ûdemy   Categories   🔍   no bake cakes

5,365 results for "no bake cakes"

Click on 5-10 of the bestselling and/or with the MOST reviews.

YOUR COURSE CONTENT

I clicked on this one as it was the Bestseller. I couldn't find a course that said it was a **'no-bake'** (maybe I've just given you an idea!).

Have a look at the course content, titles, pictures, and videos.

If this is the BESTSELLER, your course needs to be EVEN BETTER!

YOUR COURSE CONTENT

Look at the section: What you'll learn.

What you'll learn

- ✓ Different Techniques of Baking
- ✓ How to Make Bakery Style Raspberry Muffin
- ✓ How to Make the Most Fluffiest Orange Cake
- ✓ Understand the Role of Ingredients in Baking
- ✓ How to Bake Brown Butter Chocolate Chip Cookies
- ✓ How to Make a Lemon and Berries Bundt Cake

We know our course will be better because of all the research we have done. We would include vanilla cake, cheesecake etc.

This is where all the research you have done REALLY comes into play!

YOUR COURSE CONTENT

udemy

Now look at the course content:

Baking 101- The Basics of Baking- Cookies,Muffins and Cakes

Bestseller 4.6 ★ (163 ratings) 933 students

Course content

10 sections • 34 lectures • 1h 15m total length

Collapse all sections

∧ **Introduction**		4 lectures • 6min
▶ Introduction to the Course	Preview	02:29
▶ Class Project		00:45
▶ Baking Tips To be a Successful Baker	Preview	02:10
▶ How to Download the Recipe Book		01:03
∧ **Tools to Start your Baking Journey**		2 lectures • 5min
▶ Tools to Start your Baking Journey		03:31
▶ How to Use a Scale		01:43
∧ **All About Flour and Leavening Agents**		2 lectures • 6min
▶ All About Flour	Preview	03:57
▶ Baking Powder vs Baking Soda		02:07
∧ **Sugars and Eggs- The Flavor Booster and Eggs the Natural Leavener**		2 lectures • 4min

We know we need to make sure we at least cover these subjects in our course.

YOUR COURSE CONTENT

udemy

Look at the top 5-10 bestsellers and write below what they include. You are looking for any patterns, new ideas and essentials that your course NEEDS to include. Write your ideas below:

....
....
....
....
....
....
....
....
....
....
....
....
....
....
....
....
....
....

YOUR COURSE CONTENT

ûdemy

Go onto the REVIEWS.

Lifestyle > Food & Beverage > Baking

Baking 101- The Basics of Baking-Cookies, Muffins and Cakes

Take your Baking skills to the next level by learning baking techniques

Bestseller 4.6 ★★★★☆ (163 ratings) 933 students

Like we did on Amazon, look at all the reviews.

For the 4-5 stars, make a note of things that customers LOVED (and make sure you try to include this in your course).

For the 1-3 stars, make a note of all of the things that customers didn't like and be sure to AVOID this in your course.

YOUR COURSE CONTENT

udemy

Go onto the REVIEWS.

They are GOLD for what to include and NOT include in YOUR COURSE!

★★★☆☆ 8 months ago

Nice videos. I wish the measurements were included in the videos, though.

~~Was this review helpful?~~

So you would make sure you included the measurements in the videos.

★★★★★ 2 months ago

Wow. Such an incredible course. I have learnt a lot that can help me in my baking journey. And the instructor's way of teaching is amazing. Step by step and with a lot of consideration. Thanks

★★★★☆ 5 days ago

I really like the lessons and recipes my only problem is that it doesn't tell you the measurements for the ingredients in the recipes

This is another review talking about the measurements, so we definitely need to make them very clear.

★★★★★ 2 months ago

Wow. Such an incredible course. I have learnt a lot that can help me in my baking journey. And the instructor's way of teaching is amazing. Step by step and with a lot of consideration. Thanks

YOUR COURSE CONTENT

ůdemy

Go onto the REVIEWS.

Write down what you NEED TO INCLUDE:

....

....

....

....

....

....

....

....

....

....

....

....

....

....

....

....

YOUR COURSE CONTENT

udemy

Go onto the REVIEWS.

Write down what you NEED TO AVOID:

....
....
....
....
....
....
....
....
....
....
....
....
....
....
....
....
....
....

YOUR COURSE CONTENT

Do this for all 5-10 bestselling books in your niche and write down the ideas below:

I need to make sure I include the following in my course:

....

....

....

....

....

....

....

....

....

....

....

....

....

....

....

....

....

YOUR COURSE CONTENT

Write your CONTENT IDEAS from your list here (if you prefer to keep your list in one place).

1. ....
2. ....
3. ....
4. ....
5. ....
6. ....
7. ....
8. ....
9. ....
10. ....
11. ....
12. ....
13. ....
14. ....
15. ....

Get Helium 10 here (with a discount)

SCAN ME

YOUR COURSE CONTENT

What to keep, what to get rid of?

You're probably thinking 'I have so much information, so many ideas of what to put in my course, how do I know what to focus on and what to leave out (if anything?)

Head over to Google Forms - https://docs.google.com/forms

Create a survey like this example with ALL of your ideas. Send it to as many people within your target audience. Tell them they will get a 50% discount on the final version. Build the course around your target audience.

The aim is to ONLY include numbers 3-5 in your course.

This way, your course will ONLY feature what your audience wants/needs and doesn't include things they would find boring or not useful - DO NOT SKIP THIS PART!

YOUR COURSE CONTENT

What to keep, what to get rid of?

These surveys are free to do and there are lots of YouTube videos explaining how to do them, but the more you do them, the easier they become.

YOUR COURSE CONTENT

What to keep, what to get rid of?

THE RESULTS.

Things my audience wants to keep (1 line per chapter/module/idea) - they must have voted a 3 or above.

....

....

....

....

....

....

....

....

....

....

....

....

....

....

....

....

....

YOUR COURSE CONTENT

What to keep, what to get rid of?

THE RESULTS - CONTINUED

Things my audience wants to keep (1 line per chapter/module/idea) - they must have voted a 3 or above.

....

....

....

....

....

....

....

....

....

....

....

....

....

....

....

....

....

YOUR COURSE CONTENT

Our Lessons:

To make our lessons engaging and transformational, we need to know at the beginning what WE want our students to go through.

Go from this - **Not being able to bake a cake.**

To this - **Being able to bake a cake.**

Each lesson ALSO needs to be transformational so that we are moving out students along otherwise they will get bored and leave us poor reviews.

Lesson Plan:

Lesson 1 Title

My student will go from:

....

....

to:

....

....

YOUR LESSON PLANS

YOUR LESSON PLANS

Fill in the gaps for YOUR course:

Module No: ....   Title: ....

What they will cover in this lesson: ....

They will DO this: ....

They will KNOW this: ....

They will LEARN this: ....

Lesson No: .... Title: ....

My student will go from: ....

To: ....

Personal Story: ....
Theory about this lesson: ....
Relevance of this lesson: ....
Solution - WHAT: ....
Solution - HOW: ....
Practical - what they will do: ....
....
....

Call to action - what they need to do next: ....
....
....

YOUR LESSON PLANS

Fill in the gaps for YOUR course:

Module No: ....   Title: ....

What they will cover in this lesson: ....

They will DO this: ....

They will KNOW this: ....

They will LEARN this: ....

Lesson No: .... Title: ....

My student will go from: ....

To: ....

Personal Story: ....
Theory about this lesson: ....
Relevance of this lesson: ....
Solution - WHAT: ....
Solution - HOW: ....
Practical - what they will do: ....
....
....

Call to action - what they need to do next: ....
....
....

YOUR LESSON PLANS

Fill in the gaps for YOUR course:

Module No: .... Title: ....

What they will cover in this lesson: ....

They will DO this: ....

They will KNOW this: ....

They will LEARN this: ....

Lesson No: .... Title: ....

My student will go from: ....

To: ....

Personal Story: ....
Theory about this lesson: ....
Relevance of this lesson: ....
Solution - WHAT: ....
Solution - HOW: ....
Practical - what they will do: ....
....
....

Call to action - what they need to do next: ....
....
....

YOUR LESSON PLANS

Fill in the gaps for YOUR course:

Module No: .... Title: ....

What they will cover in this lesson: ....

They will DO this: ....

They will KNOW this: ....

They will LEARN this: ....

Lesson No: .... Title: ....

My student will go from: ....

To: ....

Personal Story: ....
Theory about this lesson: ....
Relevance of this lesson: ....
Solution - WHAT: ....
Solution - HOW: ....
Practical - what they will do: ....
....
....

Call to action - what they need to do next: ....
....
....

YOUR LESSON PLANS

Fill in the gaps for YOUR course:

Module No: .... Title: ....

What they will cover in this lesson: ....

They will DO this: ....

They will KNOW this: ....

They will LEARN this: ....

Lesson No: .... Title: ....

My student will go from: ....

To: ....

Personal Story: ....
Theory about this lesson: ....
Relevance of this lesson: ....
Solution - WHAT: ....
Solution - HOW: ....
Practical - what they will do: ....
....
....

Call to action - what they need to do next: ....
....
....

YOUR LESSON PLANS

Fill in the gaps for YOUR course:

Module No: ....   Title: ....

What they will cover in this lesson: ....

They will DO this: ....

They will KNOW this: ....

They will LEARN this: ....

Lesson No: .... Title: ....

My student will go from: ....

To: ....

Personal Story: ....
Theory about this lesson: ....
Relevance of this lesson: ....
Solution - WHAT: ....
Solution - HOW: ....
Practical - what they will do: ....
....
....

Call to action - what they need to do next: ....
....
....

YOUR LESSON PLANS

Fill in the gaps for YOUR course:

Module No: .... Title: ....

What they will cover in this lesson: ....

They will DO this: ....

They will KNOW this: ....

They will LEARN this: ....

Lesson No: .... Title: ....

My student will go from: ....

To: ....

Personal Story: ....
Theory about this lesson: ....
Relevance of this lesson: ....
Solution - WHAT: ....
Solution - HOW: ....
Practical - what they will do: ....
....
....

Call to action - what they need to do next: ....
....
....

YOUR LESSON PLANS

Fill in the gaps for YOUR course:

Module No: ....   Title: ....

What they will cover in this lesson: ....

They will DO this: ....

They will KNOW this: ....

They will LEARN this: ....

Lesson No: .... Title: ....

My student will go from: ....

To: ....

Personal Story: ....
Theory about this lesson: ....
Relevance of this lesson: ....
Solution - WHAT: ....
Solution - HOW: ....
Practical - what they will do: ....
....
....

Call to action - what they need to do next: ....
....
....

YOUR LESSON PLANS

Fill in the gaps for YOUR course:

Module No: .... Title: ....

What they will cover in this lesson: ....

They will DO this: ....

They will KNOW this: ....

They will LEARN this: ....

Lesson No: .... Title: ....

My student will go from: ....

To: ....

Personal Story: ....
Theory about this lesson: ....
Relevance of this lesson: ....
Solution - WHAT: ....
Solution - HOW: ....
Practical - what they will do: ....
....
....

Call to action - what they need to do next: ....
....
....

YOUR LESSON PLANS

Fill in the gaps for YOUR course:

Module No: .... Title: ....

What they will cover in this lesson: ....

They will DO this: ....

They will KNOW this: ....

They will LEARN this: ....

Lesson No: .... Title: ....

My student will go from: ....

To: ....

Personal Story: ....
Theory about this lesson: ....
Relevance of this lesson: ....
Solution - WHAT: ....
Solution - HOW: ....
Practical - what they will do: ....
....
....

Call to action - what they need to do next: ....
....
....

YOUR LESSON PLANS

Fill in the gaps for YOUR course:

Module No: .... Title: ....

What they will cover in this lesson: ....

They will DO this: ....

They will KNOW this: ....

They will LEARN this: ....

Lesson No: .... Title: ....

My student will go from: ....

To: ....

Personal Story: ....
Theory about this lesson: ....
Relevance of this lesson: ....
Solution - WHAT: ....
Solution - HOW: ....
Practical - what they will do: ....
....
....

Call to action - what they need to do next: ....
....
....

YOUR LESSON PLANS

Fill in the gaps for YOUR course:

Module No: ....   Title: ....

What they will cover in this lesson: ....

They will DO this: ....

They will KNOW this: ....

They will LEARN this: ....

Lesson No: .... Title: ....

My student will go from: ....

To: ....

Personal Story: ....
Theory about this lesson: ....
Relevance of this lesson: ....
Solution - WHAT: ....
Solution - HOW: ....
Practical - what they will do: ....
....
....

Call to action - what they need to do next: ....
....
....

YOUR LESSON PLANS

Fill in the gaps for YOUR course:

Module No: .... Title: ....

What they will cover in this lesson: ....

They will DO this: ....

They will KNOW this: ....

They will LEARN this: ....

Lesson No: .... Title: ....

My student will go from: ....

To: ....

Personal Story: ....
Theory about this lesson: ....
Relevance of this lesson: ....
Solution - WHAT: ....
Solution - HOW: ....
Practical - what they will do: ....
....
....

Call to action - what they need to do next: ....
....
....

YOUR LESSON PLANS

Fill in the gaps for YOUR course:

Module No: .... Title: ....

What they will cover in this lesson: ....

They will DO this: ....

They will KNOW this: ....

They will LEARN this: ....

Lesson No: .... Title: ....

My student will go from: ....

To: ....

Personal Story: ....
Theory about this lesson: ....
Relevance of this lesson: ....
Solution - WHAT: ....
Solution - HOW: ....
Practical - what they will do: ....
....
....

Call to action - what they need to do next: ....
....
....

YOUR LESSON PLANS

Fill in the gaps for YOUR course:

Module No: .... Title: ....

What they will cover in this lesson: ....

They will DO this: ....

They will KNOW this: ....

They will LEARN this: ....

Lesson No: .... Title: ....

My student will go from: ....

To: ....

Personal Story: ....
Theory about this lesson: ....
Relevance of this lesson: ....
Solution - WHAT: ....
Solution - HOW: ....
Practical - what they will do: ....
....
....

Call to action - what they need to do next: ....
....
....

YOUR LESSON PLANS

Fill in the gaps for YOUR course:

Module No: .... Title: ....

What they will cover in this lesson: ....

They will DO this: ....

They will KNOW this: ....

They will LEARN this: ....

Lesson No: .... Title: ....

My student will go from: ....

To: ....

Personal Story: ....
Theory about this lesson: ....
Relevance of this lesson: ....
Solution - WHAT: ....
Solution - HOW: ....
Practical - what they will do: ....
....
....

Call to action - what they need to do next: ....
....
....

YOUR LESSON PLANS

Fill in the gaps for YOUR course:

Module No: .... Title: ....

What they will cover in this lesson: ....

They will DO this: ....

They will KNOW this: ....

They will LEARN this: ....

Lesson No: .... Title: ....

My student will go from: ....

To: ....

Personal Story: ....
Theory about this lesson: ....
Relevance of this lesson: ....
Solution - WHAT: ....
Solution - HOW: ....
Practical - what they will do: ....
....
....

Call to action - what they need to do next: ....
....
....

YOUR LESSON PLANS

Fill in the gaps for YOUR course:

Module No: ....   Title: ....

What they will cover in this lesson: ....

They will DO this: ....

They will KNOW this: ....

They will LEARN this: ....

Lesson No: .... Title: ....

My student will go from: ....

To: ....

Personal Story: ....
Theory about this lesson: ....
Relevance of this lesson: ....
Solution - WHAT: ....
Solution - HOW: ....
Practical - what they will do: ....
....
....

Call to action - what they need to do next: ....
....
....

YOUR LESSON PLANS

Fill in the gaps for YOUR course:

Module No: .... Title: ....

What they will cover in this lesson: ....

They will DO this: ....

They will KNOW this: ....

They will LEARN this: ....

Lesson No: .... Title: ....

My student will go from: ....

To: ....

Personal Story: ....
Theory about this lesson: ....
Relevance of this lesson: ....
Solution - WHAT: ....
Solution - HOW: ....
Practical - what they will do: ....
....
....

Call to action - what they need to do next: ....
....
....

YOUR LESSON PLANS

Fill in the gaps for YOUR course:

Module No: .... Title: ....

What they will cover in this lesson: ....

They will DO this: ....

They will KNOW this: ....

They will LEARN this: ....

Lesson No: .... Title: ....

My student will go from: ....

To: ....

Personal Story: ....
Theory about this lesson: ....
Relevance of this lesson: ....
Solution - WHAT: ....
Solution - HOW: ....
Practical - what they will do: ....
....
....

Call to action - what they need to do next: ....
....
....

YOUR LESSON PLANS

Fill in the gaps for YOUR course:

Module No: .... Title: ....

What they will cover in this lesson: ....

They will DO this: ....

They will KNOW this: ....

They will LEARN this: ....

Lesson No: .... Title: ....

My student will go from: ....

To: ....

Personal Story: ....
Theory about this lesson: ....
Relevance of this lesson: ....
Solution - WHAT: ....
Solution - HOW: ....
Practical - what they will do: ....
....
....

Call to action - what they need to do next: ....
....
....

YOUR LESSON PLANS

Fill in the gaps for YOUR course:

Module No: ....   Title: ....

What they will cover in this lesson: ....

They will DO this: ....

They will KNOW this: ....

They will LEARN this: ....

Lesson No: .... Title: ....

My student will go from: ....

To: ....

Personal Story: ....
Theory about this lesson: ....
Relevance of this lesson: ....
Solution - WHAT: ....
Solution - HOW: ....
Practical - what they will do: ....
....
....

Call to action - what they need to do next: ....
....
....

YOUR LESSON PLANS

Fill in the gaps for YOUR course:

Module No: .... Title: ....

What they will cover in this lesson: ....

They will DO this: ....

They will KNOW this: ....

They will LEARN this: ....

Lesson No: .... Title: ....

My student will go from: ....

To: ....

Personal Story: ....
Theory about this lesson: ....
Relevance of this lesson: ....
Solution - WHAT: ....
Solution - HOW: ....
Practical - what they will do: ....
....
....

Call to action - what they need to do next: ....
....
....

YOUR LESSON PLANS

Fill in the gaps for YOUR course:

Module No: .... Title: ....

What they will cover in this lesson: ....

They will DO this: ....

They will KNOW this: ....

They will LEARN this: ....

Lesson No: .... Title: ....

My student will go from: ....

To: ....

Personal Story: ....
Theory about this lesson: ....
Relevance of this lesson: ....
Solution - WHAT: ....
Solution - HOW: ....
Practical - what they will do: ....
....
....

Call to action - what they need to do next: ....
....
....

YOUR LESSON PLANS

Fill in the gaps for YOUR course:

Module No: ....   Title: ....

What they will cover in this lesson: ....

They will DO this: ....

They will KNOW this: ....

They will LEARN this: ....

Lesson No: .... Title: ....

My student will go from: ....

To: ....

Personal Story: ....
Theory about this lesson: ....
Relevance of this lesson: ....
Solution - WHAT: ....
Solution - HOW: ....
Practical - what they will do: ....
....
....

Call to action - what they need to do next: ....
....
....

YOUR LESSON PLANS

Fill in the gaps for YOUR course:

Module No: .... Title: ....

What they will cover in this lesson: ....

They will DO this: ....

They will KNOW this: ....

They will LEARN this: ....

Lesson No: .... Title: ....

My student will go from: ....

To: ....

Personal Story: ....
Theory about this lesson: ....
Relevance of this lesson: ....
Solution - WHAT: ....
Solution - HOW: ....
Practical - what they will do: ....
....
....

Call to action - what they need to do next: ....
....
....

YOUR LESSON PLANS

Fill in the gaps for YOUR course:

Module No: .... Title: ....

What they will cover in this lesson: ....

They will DO this: ....

They will KNOW this: ....

They will LEARN this: ....

Lesson No: .... Title: ....

My student will go from: ....

To: ....

Personal Story: ....
Theory about this lesson: ....
Relevance of this lesson: ....
Solution - WHAT: ....
Solution - HOW: ....
Practical - what they will do: ....
....
....

Call to action - what they need to do next: ....
....
....

YOUR LESSON PLANS

Fill in the gaps for YOUR course:

Module No: ....   Title: ....

What they will cover in this lesson: ....

They will DO this: ....

They will KNOW this: ....

They will LEARN this: ....

Lesson No: .... Title: ....

My student will go from: ....

To: ....

Personal Story: ....
Theory about this lesson: ....
Relevance of this lesson: ....
Solution - WHAT: ....
Solution - HOW: ....
Practical - what they will do: ....
....
....

Call to action - what they need to do next: ....
....
....

YOUR LESSON PLANS

Fill in the gaps for YOUR course:

Module No: .... Title: ....

What they will cover in this lesson: ....

They will DO this: ....

They will KNOW this: ....

They will LEARN this: ....

Lesson No: .... Title: ....

My student will go from: ....

To: ....

Personal Story: ....
Theory about this lesson: ....
Relevance of this lesson: ....
Solution - WHAT: ....
Solution - HOW: ....
Practical - what they will do: ....
....
....

Call to action - what they need to do next: ....
....
....

YOUR LESSON PLANS

Fill in the gaps for YOUR course:

Module No: .... Title: ....

What they will cover in this lesson: ....

They will DO this: ....

They will KNOW this: ....

They will LEARN this: ....

Lesson No: .... Title: ....

My student will go from: ....

To: ....

Personal Story: ....
Theory about this lesson: ....
Relevance of this lesson: ....
Solution - WHAT: ....
Solution - HOW: ....
Practical - what they will do: ....
....
....

Call to action - what they need to do next: ....
....
....

Now we have planned each module/lesson,
we just need to pop it into an overview so that we can easily see what we have recorded - see next page.

You are now ready to transfer your
LESSON PLANS
onto **SLIDES** to use in your course.

You can use free tools of course, I
personally prefer to use **Canva.**

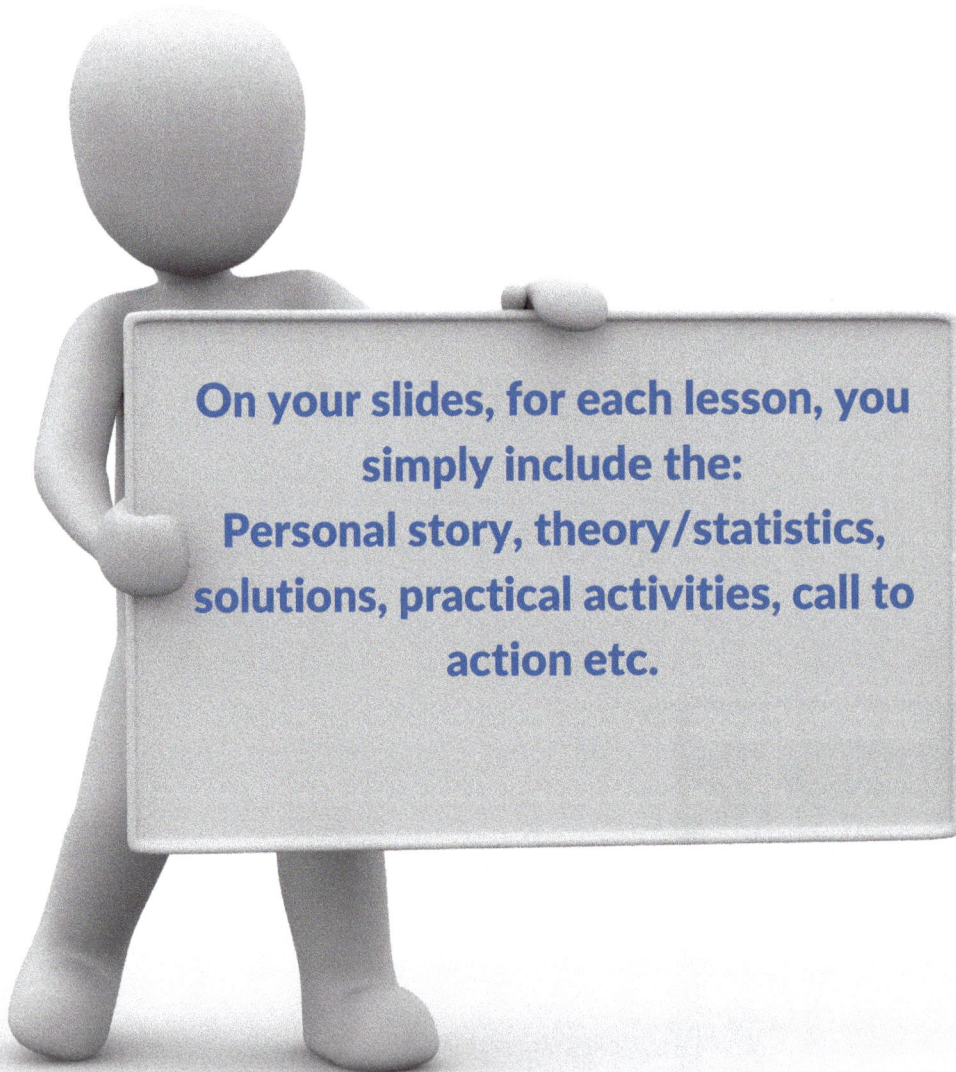

On your slides, for each lesson, you simply include the:
Personal story, theory/statistics, solutions, practical activities, call to action etc.

OUR PRETEND LESSON

Personal Story: I have had a love of baking for years...

Theory/stats: Around 80% of people say they worry about messing up a cake they bake.

Solution: The way to avoid this is to ensure all of your ingredients are weighed out correctly before your start...

Practical: For our chocolate cake, we need to get the following ingredients out ready...

Can you see how EFFORTLESS this is BECAUSE of all the research/work we did beforehand.

You will simply record your lessons from the prompts you have made. Obviously, remove the headings of 'personal story' etc.

YOUR COURSE IN ONE PLACE

LESSON NO.	LESSON TITLE	BENEFITS OF THIS LESSON (FOR SALES COPY)	TICK WHEN FINISHED

YOUR COURSE IN ONE PLACE

LESSON NO.	LESSON TITLE	BENEFITS OF THIS LESSON (FOR SALES COPY)	TICK WHEN FINISHED

YOUR COURSE IN ONE PLACE

LESSON NO.	LESSON TITLE	BENEFITS OF THIS LESSON (FOR SALES COPY)	TICK WHEN FINISHED

YOUR COURSE IN ONE PLACE

LESSON NO.	LESSON TITLE	BENEFITS OF THIS LESSON (FOR SALES COPY)	TICK WHEN FINISHED

YOUR COURSE IN ONE PLACE

LESSON NO.	LESSON TITLE	BENEFITS OF THIS LESSON (FOR SALES COPY)	TICK WHEN FINISHED

YOUR COURSE IN ONE PLACE

LESSON NO.	LESSON TITLE	BENEFITS OF THIS LESSON (FOR SALES COPY)	TICK WHEN FINISHED

LEARNING OUTCOMES

Why do we need these?

They will help SELL your course and help to deliver the transformation/outcome.

Remember, your course needs to take your students FROM a place TO their desired outcome.

It will help reduce refunds as your students will know exactly what to expect.

The outcomes MUST be measurable.

WHAT'S THE DIFFERENCE BETWEEN YOUR COURSE AIM, OBJECTIVE AND OUTCOMES?

AIM:

What your course will DO for your students.

What you want them to have LEARNED by the end of your course.

OBJECTIVES:

Specific STEPS you will take to achieve the outcome.

HOW the outcome will be attained and measured.

OUTCOMES:

What the student will SPECIFICALLY be able to do at the END of the course.

What specific SKILLS they will have learned.

YOUR TURN

Write below - What will they be able to DO at the end of the course:

ASK YOUR AUDIENCE: What would you LOVE to be able to DO after you completed a course on........? (your niche).

What will they PRACTICALLY be able to do and what skills will they have?

By the end of this course, you will be able to:

1: ....

2: ....

3: ....

4: ....

5: ....

(For help with this, look over your workbook with what your target audience wants and use that same language).

YOUR TURN

Write below - What will they be able to KNOW at the end of the course:

ASK YOUR AUDIENCE: What would you LOVE to be able to KNOW after you completed a course on........? (your niche).

What will their KNOWLEDGE be able to do and how much?

By the end of this course, you will KNOW:

1: ....

2: ....

3: ....

4: ....

5: ....

(For help with this, look over your workbook with what your target audience wants and use that same language).

YOUR TURN

Write below - What will they FEEL at the end of the course:

ASK YOUR AUDIENCE: What would you LOVE to be able to FEEL after you completed a course on.......? (your niche).

This is all to do with emotions, attitudes and behaviours.

What will they FEEL?

By the end of this course, you will FEEL:

1: ....

2: ....

3: ....

4: ....

5: ....

(For help with this, look over your workbook with what your target audience wants and use that same language).

WHAT'S THE DIFFERENCE BETWEEN YOUR COURSE AIM, OBJECTIVE AND OUTCOMES?

To help you with **POWER WORDS**, use some of the following:

- **Assemble**
- **Formulate**
- **Determine**
- **Establish**
- **Recognise**
- **Construct**
- **Craft**
- **Find**
- **Uncover**
- **Establish**
- **Discover**
- **Acknowledge**
- **Conduct**
- **Create**
- **Gather**
- **Master**

AVOID the words:

LEARN and UNDERSTAND - Your students want the outcome, NOT the process.

My example:

'Master the art of selling your products to first-time buyers...'

EVEN BETTER - ADD NUMBERS

'Master the art of the 6-step selling process in under 2 weeks!

Much more specific!

WHAT'S THE DIFFERENCE BETWEEN YOUR COURSE AIM, OBJECTIVE AND OUTCOMES?

Let's pretend you have asked your audience and these were their replies:

Question: What would you love to be able to DO after completing this course and why?

I would love to be able to bake a cake successfully without it collapsing so I don't have to keep starting over and over again.

Question: What would you love to FEEL after completing this course and why?

I would love to feel confident knowing that my cakes would be tasty for when my family and friends visit.

Question: What would you love to KNOW after completing this course and why?

I would love to know different recipes so that I could cater for all needs.

WHAT'S THE DIFFERENCE BETWEEN YOUR COURSE AIM, OBJECTIVE AND OUTCOMES?

Question: **What IMPACT is [THE PROBLEM] having on your life right now?**

I buy ready-made cakes and lack the confidence in trying something new so I never feel like I grow.

These replies are GOLD!

We can use the answers in our aims, objectives and outcomes etc. PLUS we can use them in our sales copy as we would be speaking directly to our students.

WHAT'S THE DIFFERENCE BETWEEN YOUR COURSE AIM, OBJECTIVE AND OUTCOMES?

Can you improve your learning outcomes by getting MORE SPECIFIC and adding numbers?

Try below:

....
....
....
....
....
....
....
....
....
....
....
....
....
....
....
....
....

WHAT DO I DO NEXT?

There are many platforms you can use to upload your course to.

Don't forget, you promised a 50% discount to people who helped you earlier, but that also means they will be your first easy sales!

Only record 15-20% of your course BEFORE you start to market it. Why? Because if that isn't selling, you haven't wasted that much time. Get feedback and adjust your course accordingly.

Market the outline (which you have created) so that people can see what they are buying (without you spending hours recording it) should they want more lessons etc. Create a 'wait-list'.

WHAT DO I DO NEXT?

Equipment:

You can use your smartphone or a camera on a tripod to start filming your lessons.

Here is a selection: →

SCAN ME

You can choose whether to be in the videos or not.

Some students prefer to see their tutor's face as there is more of a connection, others don't mind

WHAT DO I DO NEXT?

Slides/Presentation:

Keep your slides simple and to the point.

Avoid 'fluff' and 'filling the air' with words for no reason.

If you have branding colours, try including them in your slides.

Too many fancy things in your presentation distract your students from the facts.

WHAT DO I DO NEXT?

When you are speaking:

Pause for 2-3 seconds after you press 'record' and in between each sentence or point (you can edit later) but this gives you space to remove anything you don't need.

It's completely up to you whether you use a script. Sometimes it can sound robotic and if you have done your research correctly, you won't get stuck on what to say anyway as you would have covered all of the important points.

Smile when you speak - even if you don't show your face. Your voice will 'sound' more friendly.

If you do show your face, speak to your students, not the lens. They want to see your eyes.

WHAT DO I DO NEXT?

Basic structure of every lesson:

- Tell them what you will teach this lesson.

- Tell them why this is beneficial for them.

- Give them all of the info (using your lesson planner).

- Summarise what you have told them (conclusion).

BONUSES

Can you add any of the following after each lesson/module to give your students, even more knowledge and value?

The more IMMEDIATE the RESULT they get the better for you.

- **Checklists**

- **Templates**

- **Case studies**

- **Test**

- **Free eBook**

- **Links to other resources**

COPYWRITING

You want to sell the damn course, right?

COPYWRITING

What is Copywriting?

🔊 copywriting

/ˈkɒpɪrʌɪtɪŋ/

noun

the activity or occupation of writing the text of advertisements or publicity material.

It's basically the words your use to sell your product. It won't sell by itself.

We need to make sure we speak the same language as our target audience and identify what their pain points are.

Get the book NOW by scanning the QR code below

Copywriting is a HUGE topic! I 100% recommend you get this book by Jim Edwards- It blew my mind!

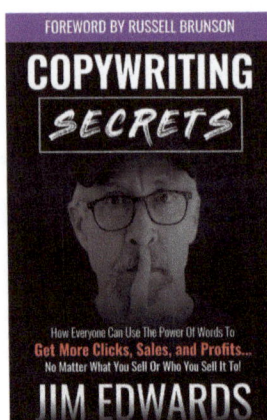

FOREWORD BY RUSSELL BRUNSON

COPYWRITING SECRETS

How Everyone Can Use The Power Of Words To **Get More Clicks, Sales, and Profits...** No Matter What You Sell Or Who You Sell It To!

JIM EDWARDS

SCAN ME

COPYWRITING

Who is your course for?

Brainstorm who your think your course is aimed at (think of the gender, age, pain points, struggles etc)

....
....
....
....
....
....
....
....

Go over to Twitter/Facebook etc and poll your audience and simply ask them!

Result: ....
....
....
....
....
....
....
....

COPYWRITING

Who is your course NOT for and why?

....

....

Go over to YouTube and look at all the comments underneath the MOST viewed videos and see what their problems, and questions are.

Write 5-10 ideas below:

....

....

....

....

....

....

....

....

....

....

....

....

....

....

COPYWRITING

Where are they?

A common mistake salespeople make is to PITCH THE OUTCOME right away.

But our potential customers may not even know what their problem is or even what they need to do.

WE HAVE TO MEET THEM WHERE THEY ARE and walk with them over the 'bridge' to the outcome.

To find out where they are, we just need to ask them again, but this time:

'What stops you from STARTING a course?'

'What mistakes are you worried about when it comes to baking?'

Type this into Google, poll your audience etc, and write down the reasons they don't start i.e. that is where they ARE.

COPYWRITING

Where are they?

Google

mistakes people make when baking | Show Volume

Volume: 0/mo | CPC: $0.00 | Competition: 0

Powered by SURFER

Q All ▶ Videos 📰 News 🖼 Images 🏷 Shopping ⋮ More

About 9,330,000 results (0.54 seconds)

Here is a rundown of the 11 most common baking mistakes people ma
avoid them as best as possible.

- You Forget To Add A Key Ingredient. ...
- You Don't Measure Your Ingredients. ...
- You Open The Oven Far Too Often. ...
- You Use The Ingredients At The Wrong Temperature. ...
- You Don't Sift Your Dry Ingredients.

Write down ALL the reasons for your niche below:

....
....
....
....
....
....
....
....
....
....
....
....

COPYWRITING

The **DREAM** goal:

If you are selling a screwdriver, you are NOT selling a screwdriver. You are selling the picture looking lovely on the wall. Plane companies sell the holiday, not the mode of transport.

In your niche, say it was 'weight loss' you are not selling weight loss, you are selling the overall dream of what that person can do once they have lost the weight, i.e. 'Ever dreamed of running a marathon?' Or... 'Want to have the energy to play with your kids in the park...?'

See the difference?

If you are struggling with ideas, simply type into **Google**:

The best compliment for.... (your niche or target audience) and write them down here:

....

....

....

....

COPYWRITING

The DREAM goal:

Examples for if you were creating a 'Weight Loss Course for Women'.

Google   🔍   best compliment for

How do you compliment a girl to lose weight?

Better Compliments Than "Have You Lost Weight?"

1. "I'm so happy to see you! "
2. "I love spending time with you. "
3. "You're so kind. "
4. "I have so much fun when I'm around you. "
5. "You look so happy, and it makes me happy to see. "
6. "You're glowing! ...
7. "You make me laugh! ...
8. "I love the positive energy you bring."

You could write:

'Looking to have more positive energy?'
'Looking to have more fun in your life?'
'Would you love to walk into a room and glow?'

This could be all part of your sales copy to sell your course.

COPYWRITING

The DREAM goal:

Turn your 'dream goals' into questions like the example on the previous page.

Write your examples below:

Would you like….?

Would you love…?

Imagine…

....
....
....
....
....
....
....
....
....
....
....
....
....

COPYWRITING

The Sales Pitch

**THIS IS SUPER IMPORTANT TOWARDS
THE SUCCESS OF YOUR COURSE!**

Poll EVERYBODY who is in your niche (Twitter, Facebook page, Facebook groups etc. the following questions)

'Whenever you think about possibly doing an online course you think....?'

What would your objections be to do an online course about.... (your niche)

What are you MAIN struggles/frustrations with (your niche) and why?

Give it 3-4 days to get all of your replies in.

Bundle the replies into 'buckets' as to what the objections/frustrations are:

COPYWRITING

Go back on to Google

Google

Type in 'The benefits of...' (your course title).

Google | the benefits of a no bake cake | Show Volume | 0 >

Volume: 0/mo | CPC: $0.00 | Competition: 0   Powered by SURFER

🔍 All   ▶ Videos   📰 News   🏷 Shopping   🖼 Images   ⋮ More

About 126,000,000 results (0.63 seconds)

Benefits of no bake desserts

- They're EASY! ...
- Many of them are vegan or vegan-friendly because none of them contain eg products.
- They're all gluten free — just be sure to use gluten free rolled oats where oa involved.
- These healthy no bake desserts have boosts of nutrition, fiber and protein.

Why are we doing this?

This is a great way to help sell the course!

COPYWRITING

Go back on to Google

Google

Write down the benefits of your course:

....

....

....

....

....

....

....

....

....

....

....

....

....

....

....

....

....

....

COPYWRITING

The Sales Pitch

THIS IS SUPER IMPORTANT TOWARDS THE SUCCESS OF YOUR COURSE!

This is my PRETEND course - *No Bake Cakes.*

These are the main objections to doing an online course in that niche.

1. Price - "I think it would be too expensive/not worth it."
2. The time it would take to complete.
3. "I bet it is too complicated."
4. "I probably wouldn't have the right tools."
5. "I bet the recipes are hard to follow."

Some of this advice I got straight out of the incredible book by Alex Hormozi (right). Scan the QR code to order yours. You won't be sorry!

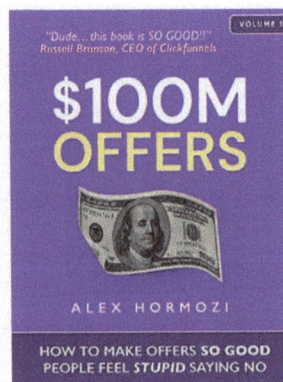

COPYWRITING

The Sales Pitch

THIS IS SUPER IMPORTANT TOWARDS THE SUCCESS OF YOUR COURSE!

This is my PRETEND course - *No Bake Cakes.*

Now, we are going to write a SOLUTION to every OBJECTION.

1. **Price - This is an affordable course...**
2. **Time - Short videos you can watch when the kids are in bed!**
3. **Complicated - Easy set-up! You'll be baking in minutes!**
4. **Tools - Using tools you already have in your kitchen!**
5. **Recipes too hard - With simple, fun recipes that all the family can do!**

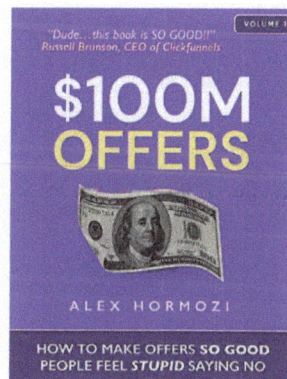

"Dude... this book is SO GOOD!"
Russell Brunson, CEO of Clickfunnels
VOLUME 1

$100M OFFERS

ALEX HORMOZI

HOW TO MAKE OFFERS **SO GOOD** PEOPLE FEEL **STUPID** SAYING NO

SCAN ME

COPYWRITING

The Sales Pitch

You're not only telling yourself what you need to focus on, but you are speaking directly TO your ideal customer and solving ALL of their problems-no guessing!

If we put it all together:

This course is affordable with short videos you can watch and enjoy when the kids are in bed. With easy set-up instructions, you'll be baking in minutes using tools you already have laying around in your kitchen. Create fun recipes that all the family can enjoy!

How compelling does that sound? And it only took me 2 minutes! You can do an even better job!

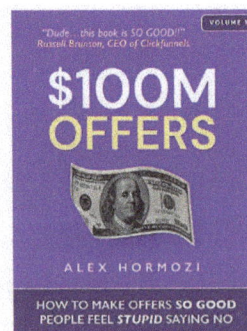

COPYWRITING

An **EASY** formula to sell your product is:

[KEYWORD] + [BENEFIT] + [WHO IS IT FOR]

Our example is:

No Bake Cakes! Easy recipes on how to make delicious cakes without using an oven. Fuss-free baking!

This is where you go over your notes and look at all the benefits and the language people use in your niche.

If you follow this formula to name your course, you will stand apart from your competitors!

COPYWRITING

Words to give it extra zest...

- Game Plan
- Code
- Blue print
- Secrets
- Bootcamp
- Challenge

No-Bake Cake Secrets! Easy recipes on how to make delicious cakes without using an oven. Fuss-free baking!

COPYWRITING

Put it all together here:

Course Title: ....

Sales copy (to include questions, meet them where they are (their frustrations) benefits of your course, dream outcome, and what the course includes):

....
....
....
....
....
....
....
....
....
....
....
....
....
....
....
....

COPYWRITING

My example here:

No-Bake Cake Secrets! Easy recipes on how to make delicious cakes without an oven!

Sales copy:

Do you have a party coming up and you want to impress your guests?

Are you worried that you don't have the right tools for baking that show-stopping cake?

Do you lack the confidence in not knowing whether you have mixed the ingredients correctly?

You fear that your cake will come out flat, right?

This course is affordable with short videos you can watch when the kids are in bed. With easy set-up instructions, you'll be baking in minutes using tools you already have in the kitchen. Get all the family after you have completed this beginner-friendly course.

With your newfound confidence, you'll be the go-to expert for any celebration. Watch their faces light up as you bring out the masterpiece!

Your course includes...

COPYWRITING

If you need help with any of your copywriting, contact me here at:

Vickytjones@hotmail.com

For a flat fee, I will help you.

Email me now to discuss!

RECOMMENDED RESOURCES

Helium 10:

Helium 10

Helium 10 is an eCommerce suite of tools for entrepreneurs and businesses to manage and sell products, find keywords, identify trends, optimize listings, streamline advertising campaigns, and more...

SCAN ME

Copywriting:

This book teaches you street-smart copywriting and how to get results TODAY! Because we all need to make more sales today . . . not tomorrow, not next week, right?

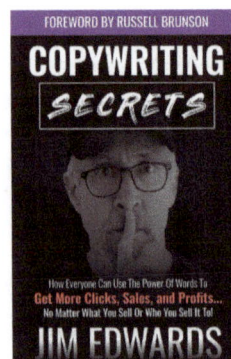

FOREWORD BY RUSSELL BRUNSON

COPYWRITING SECRETS

How Everyone Can Use The Power Of Words To
Get More Clicks, Sales, and Profits...
No Matter What You Sell Or Who You Sell It To!

JIM EDWARDS

SCAN ME

RECOMMENDED RESOURCES

How to put your offer together:

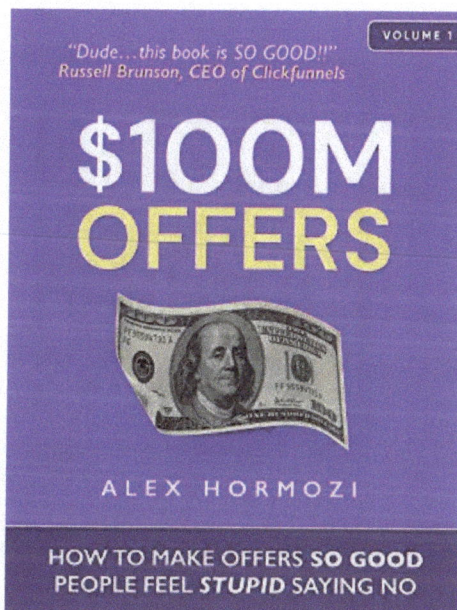

RECOMMENDED RESOURCES

Your equipment:

Grab your freebies at

HackneyandJones.com

www.ingramcontent.com/pod-product-compliance
Lightning Source LLC
Chambersburg PA
CBHW052342210326
41597CB00037B/6227